NAME YOUR EMOTIONS

SOMETIMES I FEEL SURPRISED

by Jaclyn Jaycox

PEBBLE
a capstone imprint

Pebble Emerge is published by Pebble, an imprint of Capstone.
1710 Roe Crest Drive
North Mankato, Minnesota 56003
www.capstonepub.com

Library of Congress Cataloging-in-Publication Data is available on the
Library of Congress website.
ISBN 978-1-9771-2467-8 (library binding)
ISBN 978-1-9771-2643-6 (paperback)
ISBN 978-1-9771-2510-1 (eBook PDF)

Summary: What does it mean to feel surprised? Learn how surprise
makes your body feel, how your senses spark emotion, and how to
handle it. Large, stunning photos help illustrate what surprise looks
like. A mindfulness activity gives kids the chance to practice managing
their feelings.

Image Credits
Getty Images: miodrag ignjatovic, 6; Shutterstock: AJP, Cover, Anatoliy
Karlyuk, 7, ArtFamily, 9, Asier Romero, 17, Brian Goodman, 21, Color
Symphony, Design Element, FamVeld, 5, Iakov Filimonov, 18, Impact
Photography, 19, Luis Molinero, 14, Lyubov Kobyakova, 15, Mladen
Zivkovic, 11, Realstock, 13

Editorial Credits
Designer: Kay Fraser; Media Researcher: Tracy Cummins; Production
Specialist: Katy LaVigne

Printed and bound in China.
3322

TABLE OF CONTENTS

Words in **bold** are in the glossary.

WHAT IS SURPRISE?

Imagine it's your birthday. You come home after shopping with your mom. All your family and friends are inside and shout, "happy birthday!" You are surprised!

Surprise is an **emotion**, or feeling. You feel surprised when something unexpected happens.

WHAT DOES IT FEEL LIKE TO BE SURPRISED?

Try to think of a time you were surprised. Maybe you slipped on the snow. Maybe a loud noise made you jump. How did you feel?

When you are surprised, your eyes get wide. Your heart beats faster. You can start to shake. Your mouth might open into an "O" shape. You may even scream!

USING YOUR SENSES

Everyone has five **senses**. People can touch, taste, see, hear, and smell things. Your senses send messages to your brain. That's where feelings start.

Tasting something really cold might make you feel surprised. Hearing a balloon pop can make you feel surprised. Touching something hot might surprise you.

NAMING YOUR EMOTIONS

It's important to be able to name your emotions. When you can name which emotion you are feeling, it is easier to talk about it. Talking about bad feelings can make you feel better. Talking about good feelings can help you feel closer to people.

UNDERSTANDING SURPRISE

Surprise is a very quick emotion. It happens suddenly. It usually lasts only a few seconds. Surprise can sometimes be a good feeling. But it can also feel bad.

Surprised feelings happen after something **startling**. It is when you are trying to figure out what is happening.

Usually another emotion comes right after surprise. Maybe you felt surprised when you opened a gift you really wanted. Then you felt happy.

Maybe you looked up and were surprised to see a spider on the ceiling. Then you felt scared.

15

HANDLING YOUR FEELINGS

Some people like to be surprised. It is exciting for them. But some people don't like to be surprised. It can make them uncomfortable.

No matter how you feel about it, surprise is a feeling everyone has sometimes. It's how you handle it that's important.

It can be easy to **react** right away when you are surprised. Maybe a friend snuck up on you. After feeling surprised, you might get angry. But try not to react too quickly.

Take a deep breath. Talk to them if
it made you upset. Try to turn it into
something good. Maybe they just wanted
to play. Find a game to play together!

MINDFULNESS ACTIVITY

It can be good to take some time to relax after a surprise! Try this fun activity to calm your mind and enjoy some tunes.

What You Do:

1. Turn on your favorite music or radio station.

2. Close your eyes and listen. How many different instruments can you hear?

3. Make a list or draw a picture of them.

GLOSSARY

emotion (i-MOH-shuhn)—a strong feeling; people have and show emotions such as happiness, sadness, fear, anger, and jealousy

react (ree-AKT)—respond to something that happens

sense (SENSS)—a way of knowing about your surroundings; hearing, smelling, touching, tasting, and sight are the five senses

startle (STAHR-tuhl)—to surprise, scare, or alarm someone

READ MORE

Christelis, Paul. *Exploring Emotions: Everyday Mindfulness*. Minneapolis: Free Spirit Publishing, 2018.

Kreul, Holde. *My Feelings and Me*. New York: Skyhorse Publishing, 2018.

INTERNET SITES

Emotions Coloring Pages
coloring.ws/emotion.htm

Kids' Health – Feelings and Emotions
cyh.com/HealthTopics/HealthTopicDetailsKids.aspx?p=335&np=287&id=1530

INDEX